A Wife's Little Instruction Book

A WIFE'S LITTLE INSTRUCTION BOOK

Your Survival Guide to Marriage Without Bloodshed

DIANA JORDAN *and* PAUL SEABURN

Authors Choice Press

San Jose New York Lincoln Shanghai

A Wife's Little Instruction Book
Your Survival Guide to Marriage Without Bloodshed

Authors Choice Press
an imprint of iUniverse, Inc.

For information address:
iUniverse, Inc.
5220 S. 16th St., Suite 200
Lincoln, NE 68512
www.iuniverse.com

Originally published by Avon Books

ISBN: 0-595-21786-9

Printed in the United States of America

To Donna . . .
Who shares with me the true meaning of wife.
—Paul

✳ ✳ ✳

To my dad . . .
For his great sense of humor;

To my mom . . .
For her great sense of love.
—Diana

ACKNOWLEDGMENTS

Even a little book requires big help. We'd like to thank Randy Chapman and Mel Berger at William Morris; Marjorie Braman at Avon Books; Eddy J. Rogers Jr., Barbara Mero, and Morra, Brezner, Steinberg & Tennenbaum for their wonderful assistance.

INTRODUCTION

Much thought went into the title of this book; each word was carefully selected to serve a specific purpose.

✳ **A**—This word insures it will be the first book you find in alphabetical order in the bookstore—unless some grammar school drop-out writes *A Aardvark's Little Instruction Book*.

✳ **Wife's**—Neither one of us is a wife, which makes us experts under the rule, "Those who can, do; those who can't, write about it."

✳ **Little**—If we called it a "Big" book, it wouldn't be done yet. "Little" is short for Little Pages, Large Print, and Wide Margins.

✳ **Instruction**—Okay, we know we're not instructors (see explanation of *Wife's*), but we're hoping this gets us a couple of honorary Ph.D.s.

✳ **Book**—We decided on this format after the Library of Congress told us it wouldn't accept T-shirts, bumper stickers, or match book covers.

So there you have it. Hope you have as much fun reading it as we had writing it.

A WIFE'S LITTLE INSTRUCTION BOOK

1.

GUIDE TO THE MALE SPECIES
or
FINALLY, A MAP THAT'S SIMPLE TO FOLD

Men are born with an innate ability to fold a map. On the other hand, you can't train them to fold towels, napkins, or fitted sheets.

The only reason men like canned food is that they have to use a tool to open it. How else can you explain Spam, sardines, and Vienna sausages?

Men always want to fix things. If you don't want a man to fix something, you have to pay him. You know, like a car mechanic.

Men can't stand calling a repairman. If a man says, "I'm going to fix this thing if it kills me," the only thing you can do is shoot him.

Men should not have babies. Unless they can drive it, drink it, or display it, they won't take care of it.

There's not much about being pregnant that appeals to men. Except that they could pass gas for nine months and not have to blame the dog.

Men hate it when a woman knows that they're wrong. Especially if it's before they know it themselves.

Men have simple needs. They can survive the whole weekend with only three things: beer, boxer shorts, and batteries for the remote control.

Men like dogs better
than they like women
because a dog is happy when men
leave the toilet seat up.

Most men feel that if God wanted them to use tissues, She wouldn't have given them fingers.

Men clean only what they can see. If it weren't for women, men would probably shower with their clothes on. On the other hand, this might be the only way to get them to do their laundry.

Men can't find the laundry hamper without a compass.

Women outlive men,
and it's a good thing they do.
If men *could* live longer than women,
it wouldn't be much longer.
Just till men ran out of clean underwear.

Men don't care how they look when they go out. They're happy if they get to the party before all the food's gone.

For most men, the closest they come to dieting is switching to lite beer.

Women have a lower center of gravity,
which means they have better balance
than men. This is why men get beer
bellies: If they fall over, men have got a
built-in air bag.

Men can use anything for a bathroom . . . and take pride in adding new locations to their lists . . .

. . . That's why they can never appreciate the beauty of a tree. To them, it's just a urinal that doesn't flush.

If a man gets sick, he always tries the same three-step treatment: sex, booze, and sex. In that order.

A man hates it when a woman cries because he's afraid he's to blame. And he's right.

There's a commercial where guys sit
around drinking beer, cleaning fish,
wiping their noses on their sleeves
and saying,
"It doesn't get any better than this."
That's not a commercial.
That's a *warning*.

Men carry their brains lower than women do, so when they're scratching their crotches, they're not being gross ... they're just thinking.

Men need to be encouraged to do anything common sense would dictate.

Women have two X chromosomes;
men have an X and a Y.
That's why men are always asking "Y?"
while women say "Y not?"

2.

MEN AND WOMEN
or
WHAT HAPPENED TO THE "ELATION" IN RELATIONSHIP?

Most relationships are like water and Alka Seltzer. After two minutes, you're still there but he's fizzed out.

Don't try to meet guys at bars. It's like window shopping. You know, looking at fancy clothes on a bunch of dummies.

Before accepting a marriage proposal,
take a good look at his father.
If he's still handsome, witty, and has
all his teeth . . . marry him instead.

It's wonderful when a man gets down on his knee to propose. Of course, it's even better if he remembers it the next day.

Don't ever get married on a big holiday, like Christmas or your birthday. That just gives him a chance to forget two gifts instead of one.

If his wallet contains more pictures of his kids than of Ben Franklin, Abe Lincoln, and George Washington, that means his ex-wife got all *their* pictures.

Men need wedding pictures because they'll never look happy again.

Don't let a man go alone
to pick out an engagement ring.
He'll do something stupid
like get one he can afford.

Don't marry a man who refers to the rehearsal dinner as "The Last Supper."

Picking out a bridal party is tough. You want girls who won't ruin the picture by looking better than you, and guys who won't talk your fiancé out of it at the bachelor party.

A man will never completely change
after the wedding.
This is a marriage,
not a witness protection program.

Men think the bachelor party is their last night out with the boys. That's not quite true. It's just their last night out without a leash.

Pick out practical gifts for your bridal party. Give the girls a nice pair of earrings. And give the guys fifty bucks to make sure your fiancé shows up.

3.

CHANGING A MAN
or
MARRYING A BUCK DOES NOT GUARANTEE YOU CAN MAKE CHANGE

Men just can't be retrained.
You can try, but it's like using a
mental mousse.
They stay in place for a while,
then go back to their old ways.

Changing a man is like changing a dollar bill ... what you get back always looks like a lot less than what you started with.

No matter how flat you deflate a man's ego, you still can't fit him in a change machine.

Don't treat a man like a child. Get a dog. Treat the dog like a child, treat your man like a dog, and everybody's happy.

You can't change a man.
And even if you could,
the only person who'd appreciate it is
his next wife.

Before trying to change a man, think of him as a baby, because an hour after you change him, he'll be all wet again.

Changing a tire is a lot easier than changing your husband. A wedding ring makes a lousy lug wrench.

You can't make a silk purse
out of a sow's ear.
And you can't make a stallion
out of a horse's ass, either.

Things change in every relationship. Unfortunately, one of them is never the man.

Men don't change. When you find a guy you can mold like clay, he usually looks like Gumby.

Don't make the mistake of falling in love with a man's potential because you think you can change him. The problem is, they don't make personality implants.

4.

MEN AND SEX
or
FIFTY WAYS TO LEASH
YOUR LOVER

The word "hysteria" comes from the ancient Greek word for womb. So even back then men were going crazy when they didn't get sex.

A woman can tell just by looking at a man that he wants sex. That's because, whenever a woman looks at a man, he wants sex.

Men talk about their "sex life" as if it's different from their real life. That's because one's real and the other's a fantasy.

It's a good thing their real life *isn't* like their sex life. Most of them wouldn't have long to live.

Turning on a man is like cooking a soufflé. Sometimes it rises, and sometimes you just have to call out for Domino's.

Men have so many sexual hang-ups, it's no wonder they get into hunting accidents. Before the animal even gets close, they start shooting.

Men have sex like they drive: they're always in a hurry and they pull out before you're ready.

Men treat women like VCRs. They never follow the directions so they don't know how to turn them on.

The only way to get a man to try something new in bed is to invite over a girlfriend.

When you want your boyfriend
to play with you,
wear a full-length black nightgown
with buttons all over it.
Sure, it's uncomfortable.
But it makes you look
just like his remote control.

Scientists say orgasms eventually kill men. They have only a certain number and, once they're gone, they're dead. That's why women fake them.

Don't just fake orgasms, fake crying too. Crying works better. It gets you what you want and you don't have to sleep in the wet spot.

Doctors say that the breathing techniques used in faking orgasms are the same as those used in childbirth, except the words "baby, baby" have an entirely different meaning.

Don't make a habit of faking orgasms ... although it's okay to exaggerate a few.

Men can't fake orgasms. That's why they fake commitments.

Don't think you can get a man to do
what you want just by dressing sexy.
If you do that, all he wants is sex.
If you really want a man to listen to you,
dress like his mother.

Women want chemistry in their relationships. Men just want biology. Actually, it's more like biology, recess, biology, recess.

Older men are sexy too. They don't have to wear cologne to smell sexy. They can just rub that American Express card behind their ear.

When sex rears its ugly head . . .
put a condom on it!

5.

MEN AND THEIR CARS
or
MEN, CARS, AND THE WOMEN WHO DRIVE THEM

There's only one reason why a man drives a car with a back seat. There's not enough room in the ashtray for all his trash.

A man will always choose a truck over a woman. Trucks don't mind being pickups, they come with their own bed, and they don't have a hand brake.

You can tell who owns a car
by how dirty the inside is.
Men treat their cars like clothing.
If it doesn't smell too bad,
they can drive it for another day.

Men are like car alarms. They both make a lot of noise no one listens to.

Older men are like used cars. Body's shot, rear end's dragging, and they can't keep the hood up.

If men were cars, we'd all want a Ferrari,
but we'd get stuck with a Yugo,
one that smokes, backfires,
and sits all night smelling like gas.

Men won't stop and ask for directions
because driving is too much like sex:
They can't stop until they get where
they're going.

They learned this from their fathers.
When a boy asks his father how to get
somewhere, he tells him: "You'll know it
when you see it."

A man won't ask for directions because he might find out he was wrong ... and then he'd have to kill himself.

Worse, we might see that he's wrong, and then he'd have to kill us.

6.

WHY MEN HATE SHOPPING
or
THE ONE PLACE WE GET
THE CREDIT WE DESERVE

Men don't care if they're in style or not. If a man looks like he just stepped out of GQ, it's only because a woman dressed him.

A woman dresses for other women because she's competitive. If a man dresses for other men, he's probably competing with you for a man.

There's only one way to get a man to wear new clothes. Buy them yourself, cut off the tags, and throw them on the floor of his closet.

It's impossible for a man to match a shirt, tie, jacket, and pants without help. They should mark men's clothes like those "Grrranimals" for kids. Then when he wants to dress casual, he could just look for the little fat slob on the labels.

Don't ever take a man shopping.
They shop like they're in the army:
Get in, do what you have to do,
and get out before anybody sees you.

If they built a mall for men, it'd have a drive-thru window.

If you lose a man at the mall, he's either eating, watching TV at Sears, or hanging around the dressing room at Victoria's Secret.

Men don't have the stamina for shopping. They get tired just watching the Home Shopping Channel.

Don't ever send a man window shopping. He'll come back carrying a window.

There's only one way men would enjoy going shopping: Put glass doors on the women's dressing rooms.

When men shop for clothes, they always take the first thing that looks good. Kind of like the way they choose women.

Men can't understand that women can go to a mall just to look at things they can't afford and imagine what it would be like to have them. What's the problem? That's the same reason men go to topless bars.

Men can't understand why a woman can't buy anything less than a complete outfit. To them, it's like going to buy a tire and coming home with a new car.

To a woman, accessories are clothing. To a man, they're just stuff.

Men don't understand the concept of
"accessories."
You tell a man he needs some accessories,
and he'll come back with mag wheels,
floor mats, and a sun roof.

Men can't understand how women can search all day for a little white outfit. Of course, women can't understand how a man can search all day for a little white ball.

If men really want women to read maps, they need to erase the cities and replace them with shopping malls.

Men never return anything because that
would be admitting they made a mistake.
If they don't like it,
they use it to wash the car.
Then after a couple of months,
it starts to look comfortable, so they
put it on and wear it for years.

7.

PROVERBS FOR THE MODERN WOMAN
or
KEEP THE FORTUNE, JUST GIVE ME THE FORTUNE COOKIE DOUGH

Survival tips for the modern woman:

- If it can't be fixed with a butter knife, it's not worth fixing.
- If you can't clean it with nail polish remover, it's not worth cleaning.
- If you can't return it, it's not worth buying.

Once you find makeup that looks good on you, take out a loan and buy a lifetime supply . . . it's about to be discontinued.

Don't dress to please a man. To him, well-dressed is the same as not naked.

Miniskirts and maxi-thighs go together like Laurel and Costello.

For men, it really doesn't matter
if they win or lose.
They tell lies in the locker room anyway.

Make sure you find a man
before the dating pool has nothing left
but sharks, suckers, and bottom feeders.

A beer belly isn't sexy unless it's wrapped with a thick money belt.

If you want a man's heart, go through his stomach. If you want his money, go through his pockets.

A fool and his money are the best partners in a *ménage à trois*.

The difference between a baby and a boyfriend is that you can leave a baby alone with the babysitter.

You can't get a silk purse out of a sow's ear, but you can get diamond earrings out of lipstick on your husband's collar.

There's a subtle difference between a sensitive man and a wimp. A sensitive man is a wimp with a gold card.

Silence may be golden, but diamonds are worth screaming for.

Don't listen to a man when he tells you to stop talking. Some days, that's the only exercise you'll get.

Be careful what you ask for. If you ask your boyfriend to treat you like a queen, he may just turn into a royal pain-in-the-butt.

If you love something, set it free.
If it comes back, it's yours to be.
If it sits in front of the TV unaware that
it's been set free,
you're probably married to it.

8.

HE SAID, SHE SAID
or
HE'S WRONG, I'M RIGHT

Estrogen comes from a Greek word
meaning "producing frenzy."
Testosterone comes from a Greek word
meaning "producing stupidity."

Professor Henry Higgins asked in *My Fair Lady*, "Why can't a woman be more like a man?" ... I don't know, but I do know why a man can't be more like a woman. He couldn't handle the pay cut.

It's a good thing women *can't* be more like men. There aren't enough remote controls.

A man marries a woman hoping she'll never change. A woman marries a man hoping he will.

On the first date, women wonder, *What will our kids look like?* Men wonder, *What will her boobs look like?*

As a man gets older, the women in his life become younger. As a woman gets older, the men in her life become impotent.

Men and women are alike in some ways. For instance:

- The number one recreation for women is talking.
- The number one recreation for men is talking about sex.
- The number two recreation for women is shopping.
- The number two recreation for men is shopping for sex.
- The number three recreation for women is helping the needy.
- The number three recreation for men is begging for sex.

Men are different from women. Women put on just a dab of cologne to send a subtle message to a man. Men wear cologne like a sexual foghorn.

If you send a man flowers, you're thoughtful. If a man sends you flowers, he's guilty.

Gifts change in a relationship. In the beginning you get things from Victoria's Secret. A few years later you're getting stuff from Vic's Hardware.

Women are always looking for Mr. Right. Men are always happy to settle for Miss Right Now.

Women are attracted to people, while men are attracted to objects. That's why women have nicknames for their private friends, and men have nicknames for their private parts.

Furniture is different for men and women. Men get lounge chairs so they can sit by themselves and relax. If you want to sit by yourself, get a love seat.

Men and women have different needs. Women need to be waited for. Men need to be waited on.

Women think out loud. Men think to themselves. That's because they're too busy digesting their food out loud.

According to medical experts,
women have bigger vocabularies than
men because of this thing called the
splenium, which is a path between the
right and left halves of the brain.
They found that it's bigger in women.
The splenium is why women can always
see both sides of a problem,
and men can only see one side . . . theirs.

It's a scientific fact that baby girls start talking earlier than baby boys. That's because the first thing girls play with is dolls, which encourages communication. The first thing most boys play with is themselves.

Another reason girls talk earlier than boys is breast-feeding. Boys would rather breast-feed than talk because they know they won't be getting that close again for another fifteen years.

Women are just different from men. We go back-and-forth, back-and-forth, and eventually make up our minds. Men go up-and-down, up-and-down, and eventually fall asleep.

Women are committed to relationships. Men are involved. You know the difference: A hen was involved in the eggs you had for breakfast. The pig was committed to the bacon.

Men and women have different
memories.
After a party, women remember
what they wore;
men remember what other women wore.
Women remember what they ate;
men remember how much they drank.
Women remember who was there;
men remember who left with whom.

When a woman goes to her closet and
says,
"I don't have anything to wear,"
she really means,
"I don't have anything *new* to wear."
When a man goes to his closet and says,
"I don't have anything to wear,"
what he really means is
"I don't have anything *clean* to wear."

The sense of smell is different in men and women. Men can get turned on by just a whiff of a woman's perfume. Women are happy if a man just stays downwind.

Women come out of the bathroom and say, "How do I look?" Men come out and say, "I wouldn't go in there if I were you."

Men become soldiers and women stay at home because of the way they were potty trained. Little girls are told to sit and wait, and little boys are told to aim and shoot.

Men get a better education than women because little boys are told to stay after school more often than little girls.

Men are better qualified to be architects than women because little boys spend more time in the corner.

Love means never having
to say you're sorry.
PMS means never wanting
to say you're sorry.

When a woman has a problem, she picks up the phone and calls a friend. When a man has a problem, he picks up the phone and calls 1-900-FRIENDLYBABES.

I don't know why men think they can do a better job themselves than a professional can. If this were true, men wouldn't need hookers.

Men confuse women by telling them you have to spend money to make money. Then they bitch at them about running up the Master Card.

Men think they're getting all those muscles in the gym to impress women. The only muscle we're concerned with is the one they use to write checks.

Men talk to women
to convince them to have sex.
Women talk to men
to keep them awake after having sex.

9.

COMMUNICATIONS
or
WE'RE TALKING,
THEY'RE JUST NOT LISTENING

Men think women talk so much because they want men to listen. Women don't want them to listen, they just want them to give in.

Men don't listen. That's why they grow that hair in their ears. It's like built-in earplugs.

The reason women talk so much is that they're doing men a favor. It prevents men from saying something stupid.

The three little words women would really like to hear men say are, "I don't know."

E.T. couldn't have been a male . . . he phoned home.

10.

MEN AND THEIR FEELINGS
or
THIS SECTION SHOULD BE LEFT BLANK

Men do cry. It's just that they can't remember what they were crying about once they sober up.

The only reason men show their feelings is to impress women.

Don't be swayed by a man who talks about his feelings. Find one who shows his emotions the old-fashioned way— by buying you presents.

The emotional side of a woman
comes from the heart.
The emotional side of a man
is in the foreskin.
Unfortunately, they cut that off when he
was a baby.

Men can't get in touch with their feelings because they're not located below the waist and above the knees.

Women cry at weddings because it's romantic. Men cry because they're drunk.

If you see a man cry at a funeral, it's not because the deceased meant a lot to him. It's because the deceased owed a lot to him.

Women have feelings.
Men have Feelings Lite . . .
one-third less visible emotions than
regular feelings.

11.

IF WOMEN WERE IN CHARGE
or
DIAMONDS ARE A GIRL'S BEST FRIEND BECAUSE THEY CUT THROUGH GLASS CEILINGS

A female president would clean up the environment. We've been cleaning up after men for years.

If women ran things, aside from lite cigarettes and lite beer there'd be lite men: one-third less obnoxious and one-third more like their mothers.

ONE FINAL THOUGHT

Women's role is taking care of men,
and men's role is taking care of the world.
Why don't we just relax
and take care of each other?

DIANA JORDAN

A stand-up comedian and actress, Diana Jordan has been a veteran of the comedy stage for 11 years.

Raised in Oklahoma, her career started as a country singer. Out of boredom she slipped funny lines in between the songs. A comic and writer was born!

Her hit one-woman show entitled "Female, Fertile, & Frustrated" is currently touring the country when scheduling permits. Jordan is under television contract and preparing to star in, and write, a new situation comedy for television.

PAUL SEABURN

Paul Seaburn is a regular contributor to TV monologues for comedian Jay Leno, "Comic Strip Live," and "Caroline's Comedy Hour."

He has also written for many top comedians' stage and TV performances, including Joan Rivers and Rich Little.

A comedy writing instructor and speaker on the benefits of humor, Paul Seaburn lives in Texas with his wife, Donna, and Rottweiler, Cleo.

0-595-21786-9